Daybreak
DEVOTIONS

A 50-DAY INSPIRATIONAL
READING TO INSPIRE YOUR
FAITH AND SPIRITUAL MATURITY

DR. MARY M. JETER

Copyright © 2023 Mary M. Jeter

ALL RIGHTS RESERVED.

This book contains material protected under International and Federal Copyright Laws and Treaties. Any unauthorized reprint or use of this material is prohibited. No part of this book may be reproduced or transmitted in any form or by any means, electronic or mechanical, including photocopying, recording, or by any information storage and retrieval system without express written permission from the author/publisher.

Unless otherwise noted, all Scripture, quotations are taken from the King James Version of the Bible. All rights reserved.

Scripture is taken from the New King James Version®. Copyright © 1982 by Thomas Nelson. All rights reserved.

New Living Translation. (2015). New Living Translation. https://www.tyndale.com/nlt/ (Original work published 1996)

Zondervan NIV Study Bible (K. L. Barker, Ed.; Full rev. ed.). (2002). Zondervan.

Book Cover Design: Prize Publishing House

Printed by: Prize Publishing House, LLC in the United States of America.

First printing edition 2023.

Prize Publishing House
P.O. Box 9856, Chesapeake, VA 23321
www.PrizePublishingHouse.com

ISBN (Paperback): 979-8-9862969-7-5
ISBN (E-Book): 979-8-9862969-8-2

CONTENTS

Dedication v
Foreword vii
Introduction ix

Day 1	The Perfect Power of Light	1
Day 2	Strength to Endure	4
Day 3	Effectual Fervent Prayer	7
Day 4	Be Not Troubled	11
Day 5	Dwelling Under His Shadow	14
Day 6	Tell Jesus About It	17
Day 7	Overcoming Temptation	20
Day 8	God's Plan Is Perfect	23
Day 9	Don't Dwell on the Past	26
Day 10	To Everything There is a Season	29
Day 11	God's Lifting Power	32
Day 12	Hedged In	35
Day 13	Make Your Mark	38
Day 14	Tranquility of Trust	41
Day 15	Our Thought Life	44
Day 16	Knowing the Will of God Through Circumstances	47
Day 17	Love Never Fails	50
Day 18	Learning Contentment	53
Day 19	Thankfulness	56
Day 20	My Rightful Place	59
Day 21	The Oil of Gladness	62
Day 22	Out of Pain Comes Change	65
Day 23	The Silence of God	68
Day 24	We Must Pray	71
Day 25	Togetherness	74
Day 26	He Knows What's Best for Me	77
Day 27	Delay with Good Reason	80
Day 28	Excellence in Kingdom Assignments	83

Day 29	Focused in Hard Places	86
Day 30	Salt of the Earth	89
Day 31	A Table in the Presence of My Enemy	92
Day 32	Where is the Spirit of Dorcas?	95
Day 33	Spiritual Ears to Hear	98
Day 34	Running Out of Tomorrows	101
Day 35	A Fixed Protection	104
Day 36	Steadfastness	107
Day 37	Now Faith	110
Day 38	Friendship	113
Day 39	Disappointment Guaranteed	116
Day 40	But If Not	119
Day 41	A Constant Readiness	122
Day 42	A Song in The Rain	125
Day 43	Strengthen Your Prayer Life	128
Day 44	A Godly Home	131
Day 45	Watchmen Upon the Walls	134
Day 46	Victory Through Consistency	137
Day 47	Sensing God's Holiness	140
Day 48	Never-the-Less	143
Day 49	Peaceful Sleep	146
Day 50	Refuse to Fear	149

Contact Information 153

DEDICATION

To the beloved people that have brought joy into my life over the years.

In loving memory of my beloved parents, the late Eddie and Mary Mamie Graves.

To my beloved children, Carol A. Spruill, Jerome O. Graves, and Andrea C. Graves (deceased)

My Grandchildren – Sharell, Tierra, Chaniqua, Dreia, J'hared, and Jerome, Jr.

My Great-Grandchildren – Massai, Jeremiah, and Darius

The Advisory Board – Mrs. Tracey Gilchrist, Ms. Charu Lata, and Elder Frankie Gilmore
Thank you for the many long hours of collaboration in helping this
writing to become the legacy that God intended it to be. May God richly
bless you and your families abundantly for your labor of love.

A warm and huge "thank you" to everyone who has loved, cared,
and brought joy to my life through the years.

I am grateful.

FOREWORD

First and foremost, I give honor to God for all that He has done. I am extremely humbled and honored to have the opportunity to write the foreword to this book of devotions written by our esteemed and beloved Dr. Mary Jeter.

Over twenty years ago, I was searching and contemplating my overall direction and purpose from God. My life had taken so many forks and detoured routes that I was very unclear about what was next. Dr. Mary Jeter was there to speak a life-changing, uplifting, but most importantly, customized word directly inspired by God, into my life. Every specific detail and nuance of Dr. Jeter's prophetic message spoken to me during that most sensitive and uncertain time in my life not only has come to manifestation but has confirmed the profound and sincere relationship she has with our living God.

This book of devotions is no exception to Dr. Jeter's sincerity and commitment to hearing and following the sensitive whispers spoken directly from God's own heart. She has strength, Godly boldness, and authenticity that only come from many years of true dedication, obedience, and experience with God. Her absolute love and reverence for God have led to this beautiful compilation of devotions and timely words that are sure to inspire, bless the hearts, and enhance the spiritual lifestyle of every reader.

Norman Wyatt, Jr.
Artist, Entrepreneur, and Minister

INTRODUCTION

This book of devotions has been compiled over ten years. My early morning devotions in the daily presence of the Lord inspire me to write under the directions of the Holy Spirit. My devotion time evolved into the early morning hours at daybreak. It took time to develop this discipline, but the results have been amazing. I have been able to receive inspirational thoughts directly from the heart of God. I hope this will be enjoyable as you read this devotional.

Genesis 32:24-26 is my theme scripture which says, "Then Jacob was alone, and a man wrestled with him until the 'breaking of day.' Now when he saw that he did not prevail against him, he touched the socket of his hip; and the socket of Jacob's was out of joint as he wrestled with him. And he said, 'let me go for the day breaks.' But he said, 'I will not let you go unless you bless me!'"

Jacob's past was finally coming full circle. Esau was coming, so Jacob turned to God for mercy. He prayed for God to deliver him from the hand of his brother, Esau. God had already worked it out in Esau's heart. Sometimes, good things happen to us when we least expect them. Sometimes, we receive good for more than we deserve. Jacob was expecting the worse, yet to his surprise, Esau ran to him, embraced him, kissed him, and wept. This kind of grace was completely unexpected. Like Jacob, we, too, have been extended grace and forgiveness when we least expected it or deserved it.

I pray that *Daybreak Devotion* will be a blessing in your hands as you make it a daily companion for inspiration. I have been blessed by the hand of God to give birth to this writing for the glory, honor, and praise of Jesus Christ, my Lord. It has been a joy to labor and bring forth this gift from the heart of God through much wrestling in prayer.

Daybreak DEVOTIONS

DAY 1
DATE: _____

Song of Praise: "Walk in the Light"

The Perfect Power of Light

There is something magical, inspiring, and refreshing about early morning sunlight. When the sun is just rising, and the streaks of darkness begin to flee swiftly, the sun is God's promise of a new beginning and a fresh start. The power of God's perfect sunlight moves darkness away, and God's creatures and creation are exposed to growth opportunities. If we look at vegetation and how it grows, plants clustered together don't grow to their full potential because they compete for light, water, and space.

Many of the plants will be weak and small and used as fertilizer for the stronger plants that fought harder for their share. Most likely, the stronger plants survived, thrived, and looked healthy because they found space alone to receive perfect light. The sunlight shined through its leaves and stems, and it received just the right amount of water. These plants will reach their full potential and live long. So it is in the spiritual; we can't be in perfect light when surrounded by too many wrong people. The opportunity to grow to your full potential is not possible because it's too crowded where you are. If we allow God to reposition our lives according to His will, we will be able to stand in His perfect light, and then He can shine through us and not just around us and on us.

"And the light shineth in darkness and the darkness comprehended it not." (John 1:5, KJV)

Daybreak Devotions

REFLECTIONS

Daybreak DEVOTIONS

PRAYER

Father, in the name of Jesus Christ our Lord, we thank You for the blessings of Your Word that gives us light into the pathway of life. Cover us today with your anointing, glory, and tangible presence. Give us a fresh new release and flow in the spirit of our inner man. Fill us with favor, wisdom, and understanding. Let Your love shine brightly through us as an act of worship. In Jesus' name, we pray, amen.

Thank You, Lord

Answered Prayers

Prayer Requests

Daybreak Devotions

DAY 2
DATE: May 30 2024

Song of Praise: "Faith Is The Victory"

Strength to Endure

The world we live in prides itself on strength; the physical strength of the athletic, the financial strength of companies, and the political strength of those in government and the military. When we are being hit from all sides of life, we need strength to endure. To be buffeted means to strike sharply and repeatedly like the ocean's waves during a storm. The waves keep coming, buffeting the coastline and bringing about a change even in the appearance of the sand dunes and the beach. So it is when trials come upon us, one right behind the other, it leaves us sometimes drained of our physical strength.

Our human understanding of strength is to add more strength to strength so that we can remain strong. We like to get up in the morning feeling strong, ready, and capable of facing the day. But there are times God will divinely orchestrate a buffeting season so we can experience a new kind of strength. In 2 Corinthians 12:7-10 Apostle Paul experienced a buffeting season and found value in it.

And although he begged God three times to remove the thorn in his flesh, God responded by saying, "I am with you; that is all you need." My strength shows up best in weak people.

When we may feel weak, and without strength, this causes us to rely on God even more. If He chooses not to remove the thorn, the problem, the pain, He promises the sufficiency of His grace. He wants to pour His strength into us. Receive it today.

"But they that wait upon the Lord shall renew their strength."(Isaiah 40:31a, KJV)

Daybreak Devotions

REFLECTIONS

Daybreak DEVOTIONS

PRAYER

Almighty God, as we approach the Throne of Grace, we give thanks for the power to pray in the Name of Jesus. We ask You today to strengthen our inner man with might through Christ Jesus. Build our faith so we may be rooted and grounded in love. Help us to be able to comprehend with all saints what is the width and love and depth and height of Christ's love. Now unto Him that can do exceedingly abundantly above all that we ask or think according to the power that works in us. To Him be the glory in the Church by Christ Jesus to all generations, forever and ever. Amen!

Thank You, Lord

for your blessings always

Answered Prayers

Prayer Requests

to be more close to the Lord and

Daybreak DEVOTIONS

DAY 3
DATE: _____

Song of Praise: "Sweet Hour of Prayer"

Effectual Fervent Prayer

Effectual means effectiveness that is able to produce a desired result. Fervent means very hot with a glowing effect. Fervency is marked by zeal and intensity. Our prayer life in these end times must be zealous and must touch heaven, and heaven must touch us. The great advantage and efficacy of prayer are declared in the text by the example of Elijah's life of prayer. The text states that he who prays must be righteous according to the Word of God, not in an absolute sense. I say this because Elijah was not perfect, but he is a pattern of prayer for us. He realized that his righteousness was not on his own, but it was of God. Psalm 66:18 says if I regard (if I esteem) or admire iniquity in my heart, the Lord will not hear me. Effectual fervent prayer is connected to the heart.

The condition of our hearts is of great concern to God. Well-wrought prayer is pouring out of the heart to God and must proceed from genuine and sincere faith. This is the kind of prayer that avails or is of worth. The old saints used to say in the conclusion of their testimony, "Those who know the worth of prayer, please pray for me." They understood the importance of time, faithfulness, and consistency in prayer. They understood the effectual fervent power of the prayer of faith. Our forefathers prayed effectually to bring us from the slave house to the White House; they prayed effectually to bring us from the back of the bus to the front of the bus; they prayed effectually to bring us from the shotgun homes to decent homes with indoor plumbing and running water. We can't forget how far prayer has brought us. It was effectual fervent prayer in faith that brought us thus far. Effectual fervent prayer is acceptable to God and beneficial to us.

In the text, we can see the power of prayer is the reason for Elijah's proven success. This is encouraging to us because Elijah was a man that had flaws and infirmities like us. The text says he was a man of like passions with us. He was a zealous good man and a very great man, but he made mistakes because he was human. He was subject to the same flaws and infirmities as us. But Matthew 8:17 says, "He took up our infirmities and bore our sicknesses." Then He sent back the Holy Ghost, the Paracletus, the one called alongside to help us. Romans 8:26 says, "The spirit likewise also helpeth our infirmities, for we know not what we should pray for as we ought, but the Spirit itself maketh intercession for the saints according to the will of God." And for that reason, Hebrews 4:15-16 says this high priest of

Daybreak DEVOTIONS

ours understands our weaknesses since He had the same temptations we do, though He never once gave way to them and sinned, so let us come boldly to the very throne of God and stay there to receive His mercy and to find grace to help us in our time of need.

In our time of effectual fervent prayer, we can tell Jesus, tell him all, trials great and trials small. He will bear them; freely share them; just tell Jesus, tell Him all.

"The effectual prayer of a righteous man availeth much." (James 5:16b, KJV)

Daybreak Devotions

REFLECTIONS

Daybreak DEVOTIONS

PRAYER

Father, as we pray in the name of Jesus Christ, our Lord, we first want to thank You for the powerful, effective weapon of prayer. Thank You for the blessings of a new day filled with new mercies. Thank You for granting us another day. Today, we ask You to expand our territories through the power of prayer. Grant us beauty for ashes, the oil of joy for mourning, the garment of praise for the spirit of heaviness. Thank You for hearing our petitions and honoring our requests according to Your divine will. To God be all the glory. Amen.

Thank You, Lord

Answered Prayers

Prayer Requests

Daybreak DEVOTIONS

DAY 4
DATE: _____

Song of Praise: "A Mighty Fortress"

Be Not Troubled

When we do His will, trouble will not trouble us, but we can endure and have a look-up faith. We remember what He said in Nahum 1:7 that the Lord is good, a stronghold in the day of trouble. This is a place of security and survival in the day of trouble, and He knows those who trust in Him. He knows who we are because we spend time with Him in prayer. We have a relationship and fellowship with Him. Our daily devotion and communion with Him have created a bond, and He knows our voices. Our voices are familiar to Him. He knows that when trouble comes our way, we won't panic but will take hold of the Lord in prayer. Because of this, we are not troubled but steadfast and unmovable. He knows we have to learn to wait on Him and run the race with patience. God is our refuge and strength.

"God is our refuge and strength." (Psalm 46:1, KJV)

Daybreak Devotions

REFLECTIONS

Daybreak DEVOTIONS

PRAYER

Our God is mighty, and He is our stronghold in the day of trouble. Father, we send up prayers in faith for everyone who is faced with trouble that is overwhelming. We ask You to help us to look to the hills where our help comes from. Lord, You are a present help, and we are covered by Your precious blood. We believe that no weapon formed against us shall prosper. Release Your warring angels and ministering angels into our presence. Father, cause the enemy to flee seven ways. We thank You for overcoming victory, blessings, and prosperity for each and everyone included in my prayer. In Jesus' name, I pray. Amen!

Thank You, Lord

Answered Prayers

Prayer Requests

Daybreak Devotions

DAY 5

DATE: _____

Song of Praise: "In The Garden"

Dwelling Under His Shadow

When we think of a shadow, we think of a person's inseparable companion. This inseparable companion follows constantly and watches secretly. What a wonderful way to describe the constant care of our Heavenly Father. He invites us to dwell under His shadow. To dwell means to remain constantly. It is comforting to know that our Heavenly Father is constantly present everywhere we go. The eyes of the Lord are over the righteous, and His ears are open to our cries.

His shadow is our shelter, and no weapon formed against us shall prosper. Through the presence and power of the Holy Spirit, we can live a life of daily communion with God. Our daily prayer and devotional time build a rich relationship and fellowship with God through His Son, Jesus Christ. He shelters us with His divine overshadowing, which becomes our refuge in the storms of life, our strength in times of weakness, and our great supply in times of need. Under the shadow of the Almighty, He sets up a watch, day and night, to protect Zion, His people, from dangers seen and unseen.

The shadow of the Almighty says He is always near and will hear if we pray out of a sincere and repentant heart. No matter the twist and turns of this life, we are at rest and always protected.

"And it shall come to pass, while my glory passeth by, that I will put thee in a cliff of the rock, and will cover thee with my hand while I pass by." (Exodus 33:22, KJV)

Daybreak Devotions

REFLECTIONS

Daybreak DEVOTIONS

PRAISE

My God, how wonderful thou art! Thy majesty, how bright,
How beautiful thy mercy seat in depths of burning light!
How wonderful, how beautiful, the sight of thee must be;
Thine endless wisdom and boundless power.
Holy, holy, holy, Lord God Almighty,
All thy works shall praise thy name in earth and sky, and sea.

Thank You, Lord

Answered Prayers

Prayer Requests

Daybreak DEVOTIONS

DAY 6
DATE: _____

Song of Praise: "In The Garden"

Tell Jesus About It

It is comforting and consoling when we can share with friends who are willing to listen. Unfortunately, this world can be cold and unfriendly. People are always in a hurry and hardly have time to listen to someone else's cares, but there is a friend who is close enough to be touched and warm enough to be a friend that will stick together closer than a brother. His name is Jesus. When we meet Him in the Garden of Prayer, He speaks, and the sound of His voice brings a blessed assurance that He is fully in control. So we are assured that nothing, by any means, can harm us if we are followers of that which is good. So tell Jesus about it. He has the power to turn it all around because He is an able God.

"In that, He himself hath suffered being tempted; He is able to
succor them that are tempted." (Hebrews 2:18, KJV)

Daybreak DEVOTIONS

REFLECTIONS

Daybreak Devotions

AFFIRMATIONS

God is worthy of all honor, praise, and worship as the giver of life.
As our Creator, we confess that God is all-powerful and He gives life.
We choose to live for Him. We recognize by faith that God loves us and has chosen us in Christ.
God has proven His love for us by sending His son to die in our place.
He has assumed every responsibility for us. So, we present our bodies as a living sacrifice. Through the power of the Holy Spirit, we affirm that we are redeemed, cleansed, healed, delivered, set free, and sanctified by the blood of Jesus Christ.

Thank You, Lord

Answered Prayers

Prayer Requests

Daybreak DEVOTIONS

| DAY 7 |
| DATE: _____ |

Song of Praise: "I Need Thee Every Hour"

Overcoming Temptation

Christ was tempted in all points like we are. If we learn the temptation of Christ, it will help us to become alert to Satan's strategy. We have been given weapons of warfare that are mighty through God. If we learn how to use the weapons of spiritual warfare, we will become more than conquerors overcoming every temptation we are confronted with.

We must remember that we are just flesh and blood, so we must cry out to the Lord in prayer, "lead us not into temptation." So then we must watch and pray that we may not be tempted at all, but if we are tempted, God will make a way of escape for us so that we might be able to bear it. We can go into the trial of temptation with an expectation to come out more than a conqueror because of our faith position.

"There has no temptation taken you but such as is common to man." (1 Corinthians 10:13a, KJV)

Daybreak Devotions

REFLECTIONS

Daybreak DEVOTIONS

PRAYER

"Our Father, who art in heaven, hallowed be thy name. Thy kingdom come, thy will be done, on earth as it is in heaven.
Give us this day our daily bread, and forgive us our debts, as we also have forgiven our debtors. And do not lead us into temptation, But deliver us from the evil one, for thine is the kingdom and the power, and the glory, forever, amen!" (Matthew 6:9-13, NIV)

Thank You, Lord

Answered Prayers

Prayer Requests

Daybreak DEVOTIONS

DAY 8
DATE: _____

Song of Praise: "I Know Who Holds Tomorrow"

God's Plan Is Perfect

Today God is saying to us that He has a plan for our lives. So, while we are in the process, we must stick to God's plan for us. We may be in a situation right now, but know that God has us on His mind even now (Psalm 40:5, 17, Psalm 137:17, and Isaiah 55:9). Joseph's testimony in Genesis 50:20 was, "You intended to harm me, but God intended it for good." Even from the pit to the palace, God had begun His perfect plan to work in Joseph's favor. All that happened to Joseph did not take God by surprise. Nothing ever takes God by surprise.

In times of testing, we learn how faithful God is. God is faithful and will not suffer us to be tested above what we are able to endure. He will, with the temptation, also make a way of escape that we may be able to bear it. The fact that we have problems is a sign that we also have a promise from the Word of God. It's just a matter of time before He brings us out more than conquerors. There will be times, even when we're in the plan of God, we will feel overwhelmed and under pressure, but it's just a season, and this, too, will pass. God wants us to function and focus. He wants us to be confident in His plan for our lives because His plan is perfect.

"For I know the plans I have for you declares the Lord, plans to prosper you and not to harm you, plans to give you hope and a future." (Jeremiah 29:11, NIV)

Daybreak Devotions

REFLECTIONS

Daybreak DEVOTIONS

PRAYER

Holy Spirit, keep us focused upon You and Your voice. Keep us in Your perfect will and Your divine plan as You unfold Your will and plan for our lives. Hallelujah! Thank you, Jesus.

Thank You, Lord

Answered Prayers

Prayer Requests

Daybreak DEVOTIONS

DAY 9
DATE: _____

Song of Praise: "I Am Redeemed"

Don't Dwell on the Past

When we awakened this morning, we were blessed with a brand new day, a fresh start, a new beginning filled with new opportunities. This is a gift from God. So many times, we miss opportunities given to us by God by living in yesterday. We must not dwell on the past because we have a future and a hope. Each day, we can embrace God's promises that are written in His Word about our future. God is the only one who holds our future in His hands. When He determines our future, He does not consult our past.

In the scripture, Mary Magdalene was a known prostitute, but after Christ redeemed her, she became one of the last persons to leave the cross and one of the first to discover and announce Jesus' resurrection. Because of this, she is mentioned with honor in the scripture for all generations to read. There was no reason for her to dwell on the past when Jesus had given her a future. Today, it is time to put the past behind and accept God's new things and new beginnings. So keep the faith, keep going, and don't look back.

"Forgetting the past and looking forward to what lies ahead." (Philippians 3:13, NIV)

Daybreak Devotions

REFLECTIONS

Daybreak DEVOTIONS

PRAYER

Eternal God our Father, we come in faith asking You to deliver us from the bondage of living in yesterday. Our past is behind us, and our future is before us. In You, we live, move, and have our being. Help us to be rekindled with the fire to look up and move forward in Your grand design for our lives. Thank You for helping us to discipline our thought life. We are forgetting those things behind us and looking unto Jesus, the author and finisher of our faith. Amen. It is so.

Thank You, Lord

Answered Prayers

Prayer Requests

Daybreak DEVOTIONS

| DAY 10 |
| DATE: _____ |

Song of Praise: "Leaning on the Everlasting Arms"

To Everything There is a Season

We learn that every interest in human life, whether physical, economic, political, or social, has its own time or season. There is an appointed period (a season) for all that takes place under the sun. Life does not remain at a standstill. Three words define the sovereignty of God. They are seasons, time, and purpose. God, in His sovereignty, directs seasons, times, and purpose concerning our lives. He exercises His sovereignty over our lives which means He is subject to none, influenced by none, and is absolutely independent. God does as He pleases, only as He pleases, and always as He pleases. None can hinder Him. He says He is at the end of where you have just started to go. He is the Alpha and Omega. He is the great I am that I am.

So, no matter what season you may be in this moment, God is in control, and He causes all things to work together for good to those who love Him and are called according to His purpose. Remember, it's just a season, and this, too, shall pass. So, as we patiently trust God and wait on Him, by the will of God, the Holy Spirit will open us up to face the truth about ourselves and open us up to new revelations and greater truths from his Word.

"A time to love and a time to hate, a time of war and a time of peace...seasons." (Ecclesiastes 3:18, KJV)

Daybreak Devotions

REFLECTIONS

Daybreak DEVOTIONS

AFFIRMATION

I affirm You have given us the treasures of darkness and hidden riches of secret places.
I affirm that You shall give that which is good, and our land shall yield her increase.
I affirm that I am blessed by the Lord. He loads me daily
with benefits, even the God of my Salvation.
I affirm that seasons and times are designed perfectly by Your sovereign hand for my life.

Thank You, Lord

Answered Prayers

Prayer Requests

Daybreak DEVOTIONS

DAY 11

DATE: _____

Song of Praise: "He Lifted Me"

God's Lifting Power

To take flight means to rise, settle or fly. There is something called take-off when there is a rise from the surface in making a jump or flight or an ascent in an aircraft or launching a rocket. These, indeed, are natural phenomena. However, in the spiritual, there is a blessed assurance for the believer through the lifting power of God.

We have God's lifting power available to us when the cares of this life challenge us. We have the privilege of crying unto the Lord, knowing He will hear our cry out of His holy hill. Through prayer and the Holy Word of God, the Holy Spirit will lift us into the heavens of God. Through God's lifting power, we can live above the storms of this life. This is a great comfort to the heart of the believer, so our prayer today is, Lord, let Your lifting power work through us in every situation.

"But thou O Lord are a shield for me; my glory, and the lifter up of mine head." (Psalm 3:3, KJV)

Daybreak Devotions

REFLECTIONS

Daybreak DEVOTIONS

PRAISE

Our hearts and hands are lifted in praise. Why? Because God's love lifted us. Your love for us is so mighty. In loving kindness, You came in Your mercy and grace to lift me from the depths of sin and shame. You reclaimed our souls. We will praise You for new mercies every morning; great is your faithfulness. Thank You for hands that lifted us through every situation of life. We will praise you forever and ever. Amen! It is so.

Thank You, Lord

Answered Prayers

Prayer Requests

Daybreak DEVOTIONS

DAY 12
DATE: _____

Song of Praise: "Under His Wings"

Hedged In

To be hedged in means to enclose or protect or to encircle. We have the privilege of abiding under the shadow of the Almighty. This provides a hedge of protection that cannot be penetrated by the fiery darts and attacks of the enemy without the consent and permission of our Heavenly Father. We have a well-fortified stronghold as we abide in Christ and allow His Word to abide in us.

We are God's people; our family, possessions, and concerns are all taken under His divine protection. This disappoints the enemy because he knows there are no gaps in the hedge that protects us. There is no way for him to enter in. As believers, the hedge of protection gives us peace and hope in the midst of every trial. We are confident that we will come through our test more than a conqueror.

"Hide me under the shadow of thy wing." (Psalm 17:8, KJV)

Daybreak DEVOTIONS

REFLECTIONS

Daybreak Devotions

PRAYER

O Father, every work of Your mighty hand is wrought by Your perfect plan. We are Your people, and You have covered us with Your feathers. We will greatly rejoice in the Lord; our souls shall be joyful in my God; for He hath clothed us with the garments of salvation, He hath covered us with the robe of righteousness. Father, keep us as the apple of the eye; hide us under the shadow of thy wings. In Jesus' name, we pray. Amen and Amen.

Thank You, Lord

Answered Prayers

Prayer Requests

Daybreak Devotions

DAY 13

DATE: _____

Song of Praise: "Only Believe"

Make Your Mark

To make a mark, we must have the courage and tenacity to become a stand-out. A standout is one that is prominent or conspicuous because of an excellent effort. We are created with potential and possibilities to put forth an excellent effort in all our endeavors.

The four men in St. Mark 2:4-5 displayed a faith that was focused. To make a mark and stand out, we must be willing to buy into focused faith. These four men conquered their fear and allowed their focused faith to find a way to get their friend to Jesus. The greatness of God living in these four men created a passion that brought about faith that could be seen.

God wants us to use our ability, talent, and capabilities that have been deposited in us by God for activation. Now is the time to activate our faith and make our mark in the kingdom. If we put forth the effort to create excellence in all we do, we will also have a focused faith that can be seen and stand out.

"Now, it is God who has made us for this very purpose and has given us the spirit as a deposit guaranteeing what is to come." (2 Corinthians 5:5, NIV)

Daybreak Devotions

REFLECTIONS

Daybreak Devotions

PRAYER

Heavenly Father, we come in the name of our Lord and Saviour, Jesus Christ. We give thanks to You for another day of Your mercy and grace. We acknowledge that it was You who opened our eyes this morning. It was You who allowed us to see the blessings of a brand-new day. It was You who gave us the activity of our limbs and breath in our lungs. And for these blessings, we say, "Thank You." I pray that You would show us Your will and enable us to walk in it. We pray that You would bind our minds and our will to the perfect will of God. We acknowledge our transgressions and sins before You. Nothing is hidden from You. We humbly ask for Your forgiveness and cleansing in the name of Jesus Christ, our Lord. Thank You for being our hiding place in times of trouble. You shall preserve and instruct us in the way that we should live before You daily. You promised to guide us with thine Word. Yes, we believe and receive that by faith. We will rejoice and be glad. In the name of Jesus, we pray. Amen.

Thank You, Lord

Answered Prayers

Prayer Requests

Daybreak DEVOTIONS

| DAY 14 |
| DATE: _____ |

Song of Praise: "Trust and Obey"

Tranquility of Trust

To be tranquil is to be free from agitation of mind or spirit. It means to be free from disturbance or turmoil. Unfortunately, we live in very agitated times. People are on edge, and their spirits and minds have detached from the tranquility of the peace of God. However, if we turn to God wholeheartedly and express humbleness and sorrow for wrongdoing, it will bring us back to a tranquil state of mind and spirit. When we are connected to the tranquility of trust, our troubles will not terminate our trust in God's power. Even when we are in an uncomfortable location or position, we can look heavenward. This look births hope and expectations as we lift our eyes to the one who dwells in heaven. When we connect with the tranquility of trust, our confidence in God remains steadfast and unmovable.

"My soul, wait thou only upon God; for my expectation is from Him." (Psalm 62:5, KJV)

Daybreak Devotions

REFLECTIONS

Daybreak DEVOTIONS

AFFIRMATION

I affirm over myself, my loved ones, and others that the battle is already won. You will take care of the enemy that has come against what You have ordained for my family and me. God, You have sent Your Word out, and it shall not return void. I am living in expectation of victory for myself and my family. Thank You for Your compassion and new mercies every morning. I affirm that I will live and not die but declare the works of the Lord.

Thank You, Lord

Answered Prayers

Prayer Requests

Daybreak Devotions

DAY 15
DATE: _____

Song of Praise: "Woke Up This Morning (With My Mind Stayed on Jesus)"

Our Thought Life

The real battle is against our minds. When the things we say out of our mouths are not in alignment with what we really think in our hearts, it creates a battle in our minds. Creative power begins with the words we speak out of our mouths. Our thought life is the author or parent of what we believe in our hearts. When what we believe in our hearts is spoken out of our mouths, it will come to pass. Our mind must be protected and covered in prayer because it is the road by which the enemy gains access to our thought life. It is also the road by which God has access to our lives. So it is important that we make sure the police officers of our minds are on patrol, which are the Holy Spirit and the Word of God.

We change our lives by what we think. When our thought life is centered in the Word of God, and we allow the Holy Spirit to have control, He will lead and guide us into all truth. When our thinking aligns with God's, the enemy cannot enter. He tries continuously by accusing us continuously before God. Still, when we use the shield of faith, the breastplate of righteousness, the helmet of salvation, and having our feet shod with the preparation of the Gospel, we have what we need to change our thought life.

"If there be any virtue, and if there be any praise, think on these things." (Philippians 4:8, KJV)

Daybreak Devotions

REFLECTIONS

Daybreak Devotions

AFFIRMATION

I affirm that Your Word is crucial for me to speak over my life.
I affirm I will not speak negativity over my life.
I affirm I will not speak words that will hold me in bondage.
I affirm that I will be careful with my words, for the tongue can kill or nourish life.
I affirm I am God's child, for I am born again of the incorruptible Seed of the Word of God.
I affirm I can do all things through Christ that strengthens me.

Thank You, Lord

Answered Prayers

Prayer Requests

Daybreak DEVOTIONS

DAY 16
DATE: _____

Song of Praise: "'Tis So Sweet to Trust in Jesus"

Knowing the Will of God Through Circumstances

Life is full of circumstances, and they must be placed in the capable hands of God. A circumstance can be a condition, position, or situation you may find yourself in and unable to do anything about it. This is when we must place our faith and trust confidentially in the hands of our loving Faher. When we center ourselves in His perfect will, He causes all things to work together for good. We will come to know Him in a very personal way, and we will come to know what His will is for our lives through present circumstances.

Some circumstances are providentially arranged by God. In the midst of it, God is teaching us something about ourselves, so our hearts should be open, and our prayer should be, Lord, what are You trying to teach me in this circumstance? What is our reaction or response to the present circumstances? Do we take our eyes off the promises in God's Word? Our reaction or response will get God's attention in our circumstances. If we react, we become unglued and panicky and refuse to pray. But when we respond in faith, we remain stable in the storm....our faith will remind us that God is in control of every circumstance.

"If there be any virtue and if there be any praise, think on these things." (Philippians 4:8, KJV)

Daybreak Devotions

REFLECTIONS

Daybreak DEVOTIONS

PRAYER

We thank You, Heavenly Father, in Jesus' name for Your divine power that has given us all things that pertain to life and godliness. You said, "My peace I give unto you, not as the world giveth, give I unto you. Let not your heart be troubled, and neither let it be afraid." (John 14:27, KJV) Father, keep us in Your pathway of trust and keep us in Your perfect peace in the wonderful name of Your dear Son, Jesus, we pray. Amen.

Thank You, Lord

Answered Prayers

Prayer Requests

Daybreak Devotions

DAY 17

DATE: _____

Song of Praise: "And Can It Be That I Should Gain"

Love Never Fails

Until we learn to love ourselves, we are not fit to love anyone else. When we are in the bond of bitterness, we are not ready to love. God wants to heal our bitterness so that our self-esteem can improve. We learn to love ourselves by accepting Christ's love for us and then committing ourselves to express that kind of love to others. We can flow in the characteristics of Godly love by submitting ourselves to the perfect will of God.

Godly love takes the spotlight off self and projects it onto others. Godly love is not rude, does not seek its own, and does not take offense easily. Godly love forgives and forgets and does not keep a record of wrongs suffered. Godly love celebrates others' achievements. Godly love is confident; that's what beareth all things means. Godly love inspires hope in others; that's what hopeth all things means.

Godly love creates in us a survivor mentality that will cause us to be victors and not victims, triumphant to excel in love because love never fails.

"God showed His love among us: He sent His one and only Son." (1 John 4:9, NIV)

Daybreak Devotions

REFLECTIONS

Daybreak Devotions

PRAYER

Heavenly Father, in Jesus' name, You are the only One who can bind up and heal the brokenhearted. Thank You for watching over Your Word to perform it. You sent Your Word to heal us. Today, we pray for those whose hearts are heavy and in bondage through resentment, bitterness, and anger. We ask You to stir up the love of God in our hearts and lead us into repentance; fill our hearts with forgiveness so that Your love can abide again within. Amen!

Thank You, Lord

Answered Prayers

Prayer Requests

Daybreak DEVOTIONS

| DAY 18 |
| DATE: _____ |

Song of Praise: "Through It All"

Learning Contentment

A lifestyle of contentment is a learned behavior. It is finding peace in present circumstances as well as material possessions. It is having a thankful attitude for what we already have. There is an attitude and spirit of discontent that permeates society. In fact, the world influences a person to embrace discontent. The mindset of the world is to pursue more, bigger and better. As believers, we must remain watchful and prayerful to avoid becoming infected with the spirit of discontent and greed.

Being aware that God is in control, we can learn contentment through the seasons of life allowed to come our way.

There will be seasons of being full and hungry, abounding and being abased, but through it all, we put our trust in God, who is in control of the process. Every season is for learning. At this moment, we may be experiencing emotional and spiritual disappointments, setbacks, and reversals, but be confident that He who has begun a good work in us will bring it to completion.

"Being confident of this very thing that he which hath begun a good work in you will perform it." (Philippians 1:6, KJV)

Daybreak Devotions

REFLECTIONS

Daybreak DEVOTIONS

AFFIRMATION

I affirm that I'm able to release my joy, peace, patience, kindness, goodness, and faithfulness with long-suffering and self-control to flow over and into contentment in my life.

I affirm that Your perfect will shall be worked out and that Your fruit will abound in and through me as I submit to Your perfect will.

I affirm that Your perfect will renews my strength as I wait upon You in the Lord and the power of His might.

Thank You, Lord

Answered Prayers

Prayer Requests

Daybreak Devotions

DAY 19

DATE: _____

Song of Praise: "Thank You, Lord, For Saving My Soul"

Thankfulness

A thankful heart gives God great pleasure. Each and every day, we should honor the Lord with thanksgiving and praise for His manifold blessings bestowed upon us. When we purpose in our hearts to be thankful, the Holy Spirit will help us to transfer our thanksgiving into thanks living. Thanksgiving is a continuous flow of praise and thanks to the Creator of all things. This will prevent us from developing a heart of ingratitude.

There is no other sin quite like the sin of ingratitude. In the natural, parents labor and invest much into their children's lives, so it grieves the heart of a parent when the child does not seem to appreciate what sacrifices the parent has made for them. How much more is the heart of God grieved because He sees ingratitude in the hearts of His people who have been greatly blessed by His hand? Take time to meditate upon the blessings of God in your life today. Prayerfully seek the face of God to create in us a heart of thankfulness and gratitude.

"O give thanks unto the Lord." (Psalm 105:1, KJV)

Daybreak Devotions

REFLECTIONS

Daybreak Devotions

PRAISE

O Lord, you are God; we will exalt You. We will give thanks to Your name for all of Your benefits. We praise You because You are our strength and song. The whole earth is filled with Your glory. Our mouths will speak thy praise, oh Lord. All flesh shall bless Your name forever and ever. You are worthy, Lord, to be praised. Thank You, Lord, that through the power of the Holy Spirit, we will praise You from the rising of the sun unto the going down of the same. Lord, You are worthy!!

Thank You, Lord

Answered Prayers

Prayer Requests

Daybreak DEVOTIONS

| DAY 20 |
| DATE: _____ |

Song of Praise: "In the Garden"

My Rightful Place

Through God's divine purpose and plan, we have achieved our rightful place. That place is to declare without resolve that we are more than conquerors. We face the daily challenges of subtle messages designed to remind us that we are fourth-class citizens; however, we must be confident in knowing who we are and whose we are. We must never forget the stock we come from. This includes our family history and heritage because we are somebody. We must stay focused and feed our minds and spirits with positive and nurturing thoughts.

We must remind ourselves that we are created in the image and likeness of God, and His greatness lives in us. We must rise and take our rightful place. God has a purpose and grand design for our lives.

"I press toward the mark for the prize of the high calling in Christ Jesus." (Philippians 3:14, KJV)

Daybreak Devotions

REFLECTIONS

Daybreak Devotions

PRAISE

O, magnify the Lord, and let us exalt His name together. We will bow down toward Your holy temple and will praise Your name for Your love and faithfulness, for You have exalted above all things Your name and Your word. Your name is full of power, and You reveal great truths about Yourself that can be found only in Your name. You are the God of all comfort, the God of all grace, the great Shepherd of Your sheep. Your name is all in all. Our help is in the name of the Lord, who made heaven and earth. I will magnify and praise Your holy name.

Thank You, Lord

Answered Prayers

Prayer Requests

Daybreak DEVOTIONS

DAY 21
DATE: _____

Song of Praise: "He Has Made Me Glad"

The Oil of Gladness

God is always concerned about our comfort and joy; when we have been wounded by words from our enemies, sin, and battles of this life, we need to be anointed with the healing oil of gladness. The good shepherd knows how to prepare a table of recovery and healing when the sheep have been wounded. The oil of gladness is for recovery from those seasons of wounds. Gladness means having a cheerful or happy disposition because we have experienced joy and delight.

Jesus makes us glad, and the Holy Spirit gives us the garment of praise for the spirit of heaviness. Today, He wants to anoint our head with oil and dress us up in the garment of praise so that we can go forth with a shine on our face and in our spirit. Receive the oil of gladness and be happy.

"To appoint unto them that mourn in Zion, to give unto them beauty for ashes, the oil of joy for mourning, the garment of praise for the spirit of heaviness." (Isaiah 61:3, KJV)

Daybreak Devotions

REFLECTIONS

Daybreak Devotions

PRAISE

Our Father and our God, as we approach the throne of grace, we give You praise for Your precious Holy Spirit. Today, fill us with Your love, joy, peace, gentleness, goodness, meekness, faithfulness, and temperance. We thank You for Your anointing and presence in the name of Jesus. Thank You for filling us with praise through the power of the Holy Spirit. Thank You for sealing us with Your character and nature. You are worthy to be praised. To God be the glory. Amen!

Thank You, Lord

Answered Prayers

Prayer Requests

Daybreak DEVOTIONS

DAY 22

DATE: _____

Song of Praise: "Amazing Grace"

Out of Pain Comes Change

Somehow, we think life would be so much easier if there were no pain. Our season of pain makes room for change in our lives. God, in His omniscience, allows pain to become a part of living so that we can move toward the destiny He has planned for us. When we experience emotional pain that is so overwhelming, the Holy Spirit is there to be our comfort and consolation. The Lord reminds us of His amazing grace and that He is always there to heal the pain in His own time. He reminds us that this, too, shall pass, and a great change is coming out of this pain.

We should choose to bless the Lord at all times and fill our mouths with His praises. No pain, no gain!

"My grace is sufficient for thee; for my strength is made perfect in weakness." (2 Corinthians 12:9, KJV)

Daybreak Devotions

REFLECTIONS

Daybreak DEVOTIONS

PRAYER

Father God, in the Name of Jesus Christ our Lord. Today, someone is in emotional, spiritual, and physical pain. We ask that You release Your healing virtue upon them as they bring their petitions to You in faith believing. Father, we believe there is healing for the soul, mind, and body. God, clear all emotional, physical, and spiritual clutter out of our lives as Your dear children. There is a Balm in Gilead, an aromatic gum for medicinal purposes, in Your powerful hand. Release healing today in Jesus' name. It is so. Amen.

Thank You, Lord

Answered Prayers

Prayer Requests

Daybreak DEVOTIONS

DAY 23
DATE: _____

Song of Praise: "Lord, Speak to Me, That I May Speak"

The Silence of God

It has been said that silence is golden. Sometimes, silence speaks louder than words, and only then can we hear God's still, small voice. There are times God is silent because He has spoken, and we didn't take heed. There are other times God is silent to test our faith. These are times we must wait patiently on God and allow Him to work out His plan and purpose for our lives. In St. Luke 23:9, God used silence to confound the mighty. We must be alert to the enemy's strategy during our season of silence. He wants us to be distressed, dismayed, disappointed, and defeated, but God wants us to believe and not doubt. God is developing a discipline in us so that we will be able to hear through silence.

When we develop hearing through silence, we can trust in the name of the Lord and sing as we go, keeping in mind that Jesus died on the cross and rose again so that we can be delivered and delighted in Him.

"None of us liveth to himself; and no man dieth to himself." (Romans 14:7, KJV)

Daybreak Devotions

REFLECTIONS

Daybreak DEVOTIONS

PRAYER

Our Father and our God, we come to You now with a humble heart, knowing that You resist the proud and give more grace to the humble. We ask You to have mercy upon us according to thy loving kindness according to the multitude of thy tender mercies. Blot out our transgressions and cleanse us from our iniquities. Wash us thoroughly from within. Purge us with hyssop and cause thy face to shine upon us. Wean us from the distractions and attractions of this present world. Purify our motives. Remove all pretense and hypocrisy from us and help us be truthful, unselfish, and strong. In Jesus' name, I pray. Amen!

Thank You, Lord

Answered Prayers

Prayer Requests

Daybreak Devotions

DAY 24

DATE: _____

Song of Praise: "Cast Thy Burden Upon the Lord"

We Must Pray

A prayer life and a life of prayer are powerful. Our ultimate goal as Christians is to live a life like Christ. Prayer changes us, and it changes our circumstances. When we don't pray, we lose touch with the kingdom's protocol, order, and service. It is impossible to be a Christ-like person without being born again. We are human, born in sin and shaped in iniquity. We must be born again so that new life can begin in us.

With this new life comes a prayer life that connects us with the secret of power. Prayer will inspire us to do the work of God with all diligence. Prayer gives us the strength to endure. If we don't pray, we won't stay. (1) We won't stay in touch with God. (2) We won't abide in Christ Jesus. (3) We won't stay under the control of the Holy Spirit. Let us not be so easily distracted from a life of prayer. A consistent prayer life breaks the cycle of worry, frustration, fear, oppression, and depression. We must pray.

"When you pray.... Pray to your father, who is unseen." (Matthew 6:6, NIV)

Daybreak DEVOTIONS

REFLECTIONS

Daybreak DEVOTIONS

PRAYER

Almighty God, You are the maker of heaven and earth. Thank You, Jesus, for Your example of surrendering all to the Father. We confess that we, at times, have resisted Your will and have been slow to surrender all. We confess that we have not loved You with all our heart, soul, and strength. And, we have not loved our neighbors as ourselves. We ask for your forgiveness and cleansing through the precious blood of Christ. Help us to change. Give us a heart like thine. Father, allow enough tears in our lives to keep our hearts tender, enough hurts to keep us in touch with empathy, and enough failures to keep us depending on You. We will continue in prayer. The end of worry is prayer, and the end of prayer is peace. Amen!

Thank You, Lord

Answered Prayers

Prayer Requests

Daybreak Devotions

DAY 25

DATE: _____

Song of Praise: "We Have Come Into His House"

Togetherness

Togetherness was in the mind of Jesus as he prayed in St. John 17:11, 22. Togetherness is essential to a basketball, baseball, hockey, swim team, etc. Togetherness can be useful in relationships as well as serving in kingdom assignments. There is no "I" in the word team. A team is a number of persons associated together in work or activity. Teamwork means that several associates do the work, with each doing a part but all subordinately personal prominence to the efficiency of the whole.

As a whole, we can be gathered together in the assembly (Hebrews 10:25) and in the spirit (Acts 4:32). When we are knitted together (Colossians 2:2, 19), we don't become unraveled by gossip, envy, jealousy, hatred and an uncooperative attitude. When we are fitly framed together, we become a spiritual habitation for God that leads to growth. When we are perfectly joined together, we speak the same thing, which weakens the spirit of division and favoritism.

"Behold, how good and pleasant it is for brethren to dwell together in unity!" (Psalm 133:1, KJV)

Daybreak Devotions

REFLECTIONS

Daybreak Devotions

PRAISE

Father, with a joyful heart, we pour out our ardent praise to You for the love that binds us together. Thank You for the fellowship with one another. We praise You for making me better. Bind us together with cords that cannot be broken. There is only one God; there is only one body. That's why we can sing praises unto your Holy Name. Praise Him, Praise Him, strength and honor, give to His holy name.

Thank You, Lord

Answered Prayers

Prayer Requests

DAY 26
DATE: _____

Song of Praise: "My Faith Looks Up To Thee"

He Knows What's Best for Me

The higher ways of God are hard to grasp with our finite minds. Finite means limited. We are so limited when it comes to the higher ways and thoughts of our great God. Because He is God and He is in control, we can trust Him wholeheartedly. He is the planner, and He has the master plan. Because of this, we can place our needs before Him in faith and confidence. He has our highest good in mind. He really knows what's best for us.

In confidence, we must be willing to submit ourselves to His divine care and allow Him to order our steps by His Word. He has our future in His powerful hand. Our tomorrows are hidden from us; they are distanced from us, but because He knows what's best for us, He will guide us with His eyes. You may be challenged today by overwhelming circumstances. Trust God and meditate on His Word both day and night. We cannot always make sense of our circumstances, but we can depend on God to bring us out more than a conqueror because He knows what's best for us.

"Let's fix our eyes on Jesus." (Hebrews 12:2, NIV)

Daybreak Devotions

REFLECTIONS

Daybreak Devotions

PRAISE

Father, in Jesus' name, we offer praise to Your glorious name. You have put a new song in our mouths, even praise unto God: Many shall see it, fear, and trust in the Lord. Many, O Lord my God, are your wonderful works and Your thoughts which are toward us.

They cannot be reckoned up in order unto thee: if I declare and speak of them, they are more than can be numbered. But as for me, I am poor and needy; may the Lord think of me. We praise You for being our helper and our deliverer. (Psalm 40:17)

Thank You, Lord

Answered Prayers

Prayer Requests

Daybreak DEVOTIONS

DAY 27
DATE: _____

Song of Praise: "I Will Trust in the Lord"

Delay with Good Reason

Our faith can be tested at times when there is a delay in the answer to prayer. During times of delay, we must press in and hold fast to the promises of God in His Word. We must remember that God is in control, and sometimes God has a set time to release the answer to prayer. In our waiting time, He is at work building our faith, strengthening our integrity, and refining our character.

Time is in God's control, but we are controlled by time. So a day, a week, a month, a year seems long to us. Since God controls time, He can move in a second, moment, or instant. Trust Him and know that delay is not denial.

"Because we trust in the living God, who is the savior of all men." (1 Timothy 4:10, NIV)

Daybreak Devotions

REFLECTIONS

Daybreak Devotions

AFFIRMATION

When I pass through the waters, God will be with me. In God, I have put my trust; I will not fear.
When I pass through the rivers, they will not sweep over me.
In God, I have put my trust; I will not fear.
When I walk through the fire, I will not be burned; the flames will not set me ablaze.
In God, I have put my trust; I will not fear. In God, whose
Word I praise; in God, I trust and am not afraid.

Thank You, Lord

Answered Prayers

Prayer Requests

DAY 28

Song of Praise: "Leaning On the Everlasting Arms"

Excellence in Kingdom Assignments

Excellence is good anywhere. Many times people do their best as long as circumstances reward their efforts. But what happens when we have a boss that is not so nice, or the company we work for seems satisfied with mediocrity? What happens when we are treated unfairly? Are we willing to maintain a standard of excellence in spite of?

An assignment is a specific task or amount of work that places an individual in a positive office or post. An assignment brings with it certain responsibilities and timeframes geared toward completion. There is a difference between secular assignments and divine kingdom assignments.

When one is given a kingdom assignment, it is preparation for promotion. God's purpose and plan in the assignment are to promote spiritual and natural growth and development. With every kingdom assignment is an element of suffering. We become God's publicity when we endure and go through in our assignments.

Suffering is the ability to be able to endure hardship under pressure and yet be able to fulfill with excellence our God-given kingdom assignment. Through total commitment to God, we will experience excellence and success in fulfilling our kingdom assignment.

"You have made Him to have dominion over the works of your hand." (Psalm 8:6, NIV)

Daybreak DEVOTIONS

REFLECTIONS

Daybreak DEVOTIONS

AFFIRMATION

"Once a task is begun, never leave it till it's done. Be the labor great or small, do it well, or not at all." -Author Unknown

Taught to me by my dear mother, Mrs. Mary Mamie Brown-Graves
September 25, 1906 - July 3, 1982

May you continue to rest well in His presence.

Thank You, Lord

Answered Prayers

Prayer Requests

Daybreak DEVOTIONS

DAY 29

DATE: _____

Song of Praise: "Faith is the Victory"

Focused in Hard Places

There is a reason and a season for hard places. God's plan is for us to be focused when our kingdom assignments include hard places. To be focused means having a clear-cut, precise, moving-forward mindset. When we are focused, we have clarity of perception, and we can discern seasons in our lives with the help of the Holy Spirit. Clarity of perception helps us to become progressive thinkers. We must protect our minds and avoid becoming victims of mental pollution.

The mind is valuable. We must take the initiative to guard our eyes and ears because they are the gateway to the mind. What we think has a direct impact on our attitude and behavior. Attitudes and behavior are contagious, and attitudes determine altitudes. This world's environment creates mental pollution, which brings forth wrong desires, and if we meditate on wrong desires for too long, it will bring forth wrong actions. This will cause us to lose our focus, and we will not be able to function in hard places.

Life brings hard places to all of us. In those times, we must lean on Jesus. Life is filled with so many swift, sudden, and unexpected transitions that can really put pressure on us, but through prayer and the Holy Spirit, God will work it all out. Pressure in hard places will produce principles, and principles will produce integrity, and integrity will produce character.

"This is the victory that has overcome this world, even our faith." (1 John 5:4, NIV)

Daybreak DEVOTIONS

REFLECTIONS

Daybreak Devotions

PRAYER

Father, as we come to You in Jesus' name, help us to be strong in heart, full of courage, focused, and fearless! Knowing that You care for us like no one else. We belong to You. Thank You for strength and endurance in the midst of hard trials and tests. Help our faith to be unwavering. We believe that You can do everything. Nothing is impossible with You. Thank You for Your touch today in renewing our strength. Amen!

Thank You, Lord

Answered Prayers

Prayer Requests

Daybreak DEVOTIONS

DAY 30
DATE: _____

Song of Praise: "His Name is Wonderful"

Salt of the Earth

Salt is the secret ingredient. Although it is not always visible, you know when it is or isn't there. Salt has a life of its own. The ways of salt run deep. Salt penetrates and overrules all things bitter. As Christians, we are to have an influence on the world. If we are as we should be, we can be considered good salt, very useful and necessary. Our lives should be seasoned with the Gospel and the salt of grace so that our words and actions will affect those we encounter daily.

Christ sent forth His disciples by His Word and doctrine to season mankind lying in ignorance and wickedness. As His disciples, we must strive to be salty, which means strong in the Lord. If not, we will become salt that has lost its savor.

"Ye are the salt of the earth." (Matthew 5:13, KJV)

Daybreak Devotions

REFLECTIONS

Daybreak DEVOTIONS

PRAYER

Dear Heavenly Father, we ask in Jesus' name for Your help in keeping us from harboring revengeful thoughts against anyone. Help us put on Christ and take off everything opposed to Christ. We need Your help in putting on the whole armor of God to be able to stand against the wiles of the devil. Cover us in Your blood, and let the Holy Spirit be our guide continuously. Oh, how we need Your wisdom to wear Christ so that God may accept us. Thank You, Jesus, for Your shed blood on Calvary that has made us accepted. To God be all the glory. In Jesus' name, we pray. Amen!

Thank You, Lord

Answered Prayers

Prayer Requests

DAY 31
DATE: _____

Song of Praise: "Here At Thy Table"

A Table in the Presence of My Enemy

God is able to set up a spiritual feast in the presence of our enemy. When we set our hearts to please God, we will become an offense to many people; we will be marked as a target by the forces of evil.

However, we can have a blessed assurance that we are kept by the mighty hand of God. God's covenant promises in His Word give us everything we need to win. Sometimes the enemy comes in like a flood, and we may feel overwhelmed, but then the Holy Spirit reminds us to cast all of our cares upon Him, for He cares for us. It is during those times we find comfort and strength to endure.

God prepares a table in the presence of the enemy. We can feast at the table of our Shepherd, the Lord Jesus Christ, who restores our souls. He makes us lie down by the still waters. In times of turbulence and trouble, He will lead us to be still and know He is God. By faith, come to the table; there is room for you. Believe His Word and take a seat at the heavenly table.

"Thou preparest a table before me." (Psalm 23:5a, KJV)

Daybreak Devotions

REFLECTIONS

Daybreak Devotions

PRAYER

Father, we ask You to continue to cause Your face to shine upon us. Pardon us for all our sins. We need Your grace and blessings. Everything that we have, everything that we need, comes from You. God shall supply all our needs according to His riches in glory by Christ Jesus. Help us each and every day to trust Your sufficiency and Your abundance. In Jesus' name, we pray. Amen.

Thank You, Lord

Answered Prayers

Prayer Requests

Daybreak DEVOTIONS

DAY 32
DATE: _____

Song of Praise: "May the Works I've Done Speak for Me"

Where is the Spirit of Dorcas?

Dorcas was a Proverbs 31 woman. Her hands were full of good works. Her head was clear, and right thinking gave her a focus for others and not just for herself. Her heart was filled with charity for others. Her hands, heart, and head were united together in the business of helping others. She was not a woman given to idleness. She was full of alms and deeds. She was created with God's talent to make coats and garments that blessed the body of Christ. Where is the spirit of Dorcas?

So many sit idle, and their gifts and talents lie dormant within them. God has given us talent and potential. Why are we not using our gifts and talents to help others today? Why not leave a legacy of works that will speak forever?

"In the city of Joppa, there was a woman named Dorcas, a believer who was always doing kind things for others, especially for the poor." (Acts 9:36, KJV)

Daybreak Devotions

REFLECTIONS

Daybreak DEVOTIONS

AFFIRMATION

In Christ, we are covered by the blood. We are doers and hearers of the Word of God. We are a channel for being a blessing to others. Our storehouses are blessed. We are the head and not the tail. No weapon formed against us shall prosper, and every tongue which rises against us in judgment, You shall condemn. This is the heritage of the servants of the Lord, and their righteousness is from Me, says the Lord. Amen, and it is so!

Thank You, Lord

Answered Prayers

Prayer Requests

Daybreak Devotions

DAY 33
DATE: _____

Song of Praise: "Where He Leads Me"

Spiritual Ears to Hear

It takes spiritual ears to grasp some basic truths of the Bible. Faith is a basic truth of the Bible. First, it tells us that God exists, and we must believe that He is (Hebrews 11:6). When we come to the understanding of the existence of God, the Holy Spirit opens our spiritual ears to hear the voice of God. When our spiritual ears become open, the clarity of His voice will proclaim His greatness. God speaks to us through nature, consciousness, and His Word.

In nature, the heavens, the moon, and the stars are the work of His fingers. We hear the voice of God through the birds singing, the rain falling upon the rooftops, and the wind blowing through the treetops. If we listen closely, we can hear the voice of God in the cry of a newborn baby. We just need spiritual ears to hear. Spiritual receptivity is important. It keeps the lines between right and wrong from becoming blurred. Blessings and prosperity are in place for the people of God when we allow the Holy Spirit to restore unto us spiritual ears to hear.

"My sheep listen to my voice; I know them, and they follow me." (John 10:27, NIV)

Daybreak DEVOTIONS

REFLECTIONS

Daybreak DEVOTIONS

PRAYER

Father, as we come before You in prayer, we recognize that you are worthy to receive all glory, honor, and praise. We pray that the Holy Spirit will help us in this time of prayer. Thank You for Your lovingkindness and tender mercies. Thank You for Your providence and provision. We are thankful that our sins have been cleansed through the precious blood of Christ. Oh, give thanks unto the Lord, for He is good. Surely goodness and mercy shall follow us all the days of our lives, and we shall dwell in the house of the Lord forever. Praise Him! In Jesus' name, we pray. Amen.

Thank You, Lord

Answered Prayers

Prayer Requests

Daybreak DEVOTIONS

DAY 34
DATE: _____

Song of Praise: "Just a Closer Walk With Thee"

Running Out of Tomorrows

Procrastination is the enemy of progress. We often hear the expression, "Don't put off for tomorrow what you can do today." When the spirit of procrastination overtakes us, we will soon realize our perspective of time becomes blurred. Time is of the essence. Since we are under the control of time, we only have right now. Tomorrow is not promised to us. Therefore, God wants us to be mindful of using our time wisely and realize that we can run out of tomorrows.

Procrastination is a delay for a later time. Sometimes we can become discouraged by setbacks, reversals, disappointments, failure, etc. But, we must not allow any of these to cause us to get stuck in procrastination and develop the mind of "maybe I'll just wait until tomorrow." In the meantime, opportunities for greatness slowly slip away from us.

We should not be dismayed by life's challenges nor let procrastination remove our motivation, but be all we can be today. The tomorrows may never come, but we have right now.

"Walk in wisdom toward them that are without, redeeming the time." (Colossians 4:5, KJV)

Daybreak Devotions

REFLECTIONS

Daybreak DEVOTIONS

PRAYER

Our Father and our God, as we come to you boldly, thank You that we can dwell in the secret place of the Most High. We thank You that our children, grandchildren, and great-grandchildren can abide under the shadow of the Almighty. We thank You for covering our family and keeping them safe from dangers seen and unseen. Thank You for giving your angels charge over us to keep us in all ways. We thank You that when we call on your powerful name, You will answer us and be with us in trouble. In Jesus' name, we pray, Amen.

Thank You, Lord

Answered Prayers

Prayer Requests

Daybreak Devotions

DAY 35

DATE: _____

Song of Praise: "All Night, All Day (Angels Watching Over Me)"

A Fixed Protection

God wants us to be aware of the host of angels that always encamp round about us. When we speak of encamping, it means the heavenly host or heavenly troops that are divinely placed in a fixed position for the believers' fixed protection. The heavenly host does not come and go to pay us transient visits, but they are fixed in position. We cannot see angels, but more importantly, they see us and are with us at all times and in all situations. They are constantly vigilant and aware of our surroundings even when we are not.

Each and every day, we pass through dangers seen and unseen, but because God is in control and He has angels on assignment, we can have peace that surpasses all understanding. This peace lets us know God will take care of us. So today, rest in a blessed assurance knowing that we have a fixed protection because of the Heavenly Father's provision for us.

"For He shall give his angels charge over thee, to keep thee in all thy ways." (Psalm 91:11, KJV)

Daybreak Devotions

REFLECTIONS

Daybreak DEVOTIONS

PRAISE

Today, we have the blessed assurance that we can draw near to You with a true heart in full assurance of faith. What a fellowship, what a joy divine to know that we can lean on Your everlasting arms. We praise You because we are Children of the King, and You have riches untold. No good thing will He withhold from them that walk upright before Him. We will extol thee, my God, O King of Kings and Lord of Lords. Great is the Lord and greatly to be praised, and His greatness is unsearchable. Praise the Lord, for the Lord is good.

Thank You, Lord

Answered Prayers

Prayer Requests

Daybreak DEVOTIONS

DAY 36
DATE: _____

Song of Praise: "Spirit of the Living God"

Steadfastness

Our growth in spiritual maturity should produce a firmness in our faith as we grow in the knowledge of our Lord and Savior, Jesus Christ. Being determined to remain stable in uncertain times requires us to set our faces like flint. By faith, we can be sure and unfaltering in steadfastness. We can be sure that God will fulfill His purpose and plan for our lives. The Holy Spirit has been given to us as a keeper and a guide. He will keep us from becoming easily disturbed or upset.

When we pray and allow Him to lead and guide us into all truth, we will set our face like flint and stay firmly fixed in the place of faith. (Flint is a hard type of rock that produces a small piece of burning material (called a spark) when it is hit by steel.)

So today, take courage and stand firm in doing the right thing. Move forward in the promises of God and watch God work in your favor.

"Be strong and steady, always abounding in the Lord's work." (1 Corinthians 15:58, NLT)

Daybreak Devotions

REFLECTIONS

Daybreak DEVOTIONS

PRAISE

I will praise thee, O Lord, among the people. I will sing unto thee among the nations, for Your mercy is great. I praise You for Your saving help. Be exalted, O God, above the heavens; let Your glory be over all the earth. I will praise You because You are awesome. You are the great King over all the earth. Sing praises to God; sing praises to our King. God, You reign over the nations. You are seated on Your heavenly throne. Great is the Lord and most worthy of praise. (Psalm 57: 9-11)

Thank You, Lord

Answered Prayers

Prayer Requests

Daybreak Devotions

DAY 37

DATE: _____

Song of Praise: "Faith is the Victory"

Now Faith

There are two important facts found in the scripture about faith; first, it has substance, and second, there is evidence. In the United States, we do business with dollars. In Europe, business is conducted in Euros. Both have substance and evidence. In the kingdom of God, faith is the coin we use to do business with God. So, we can say that faith is substance and evidence fueled by the Word of God. Faith must be connected to hope. If we're not hoping for anything, we don't need faith. What is hope? It is a confident expectation. We must have faith anchored in the Word of God to face the mountains of this life.

We must be fully persuaded that if God said it, He would do it. Faith that is the size of a mustard seed has the potential and power to move mountains. Faith-filled words spoken over circumstances will create a miracle. Mustard seed faith is now faith. Seeds have the potential to grow into something bigger, so we must believe God and protect our now faith at all costs. Without faith, it is impossible to please God. We must believe that He is and that He is a rewarder of those that diligently seek Him.

"Now faith is the substance of things hoped for, the evidence of things not seen." (Hebrews 11:1, KJV)

Daybreak Devotions

REFLECTIONS

Daybreak Devotions

AFFIRMATION

The Lord is my Shepherd; I lack nothing.
He makes me lie down in green pastures; He leads me beside still waters. He refreshes my soul.
He guides me along the right paths, for His name's sake.
Even thou I walk through the darkest valley, I will fear no evil, for You
are with me. Your rod and Your staff, they comfort me.
You prepare a table before me in the presence of my enemies.
You anoint my head with oil; my cup overflows.
Surely your goodness and love will follow me all the days of my
life. And I will dwell in the house of the Lord forever.
Psalm 23 - A Psalm of David

Thank You, Lord

Answered Prayers

Prayer Requests

Daybreak Devotions

DAY 38

DATE: _____

Song of Praise: "There's Not a Friend Like the Lowly Jesus"

Friendship

A friend is defined as being one attached by affection or esteem. A favored companion that is not hostile. The proof and product of friendship is love, and the bond of love in friendship is important. Love will reflect itself in kindness, in sharing, and in being concerned. To be called friends carries with it great responsibility.

Christ showed us the highest proof of friendship by showing His kindness towards us through His death on the cross. Through His sacrifice at Calvary, He positioned us in relationship and fellowship to become His friends. He said I no longer call you servants, for a master doesn't confide in His servants; now you are my friends, proved by the fact that I have told you everything the Father told me.

It is important to value your relationship and fellowship with the Lord Jesus Christ. Also, value those friendships in your life that God has created. Being a friend carries great responsibility, and with the love of God in our hearts, we can maintain lifelong friendships.

"A man that hath friends must shew himself friendly: And there is a friend that sticketh closer than a brother. Proverbs 18:24 man that hath friends must shew himself friendly: And there is a friend that sticketh closer than a brother." (Proverbs 18:24, KJV)

Daybreak Devotions

REFLECTIONS

Daybreak DEVOTIONS

PRAISE

How good it is to sing praises to our God, how pleasant and fitting to praise Him.
Sing to the Lord with grateful praise, make music to our God with your voice,
He covers the sky with clouds. He supplies the earth with rain and makes grass grow on the hills.
Praise the Lord from the earth. Let us praise the name of the Lord, for His name
alone is exalted. Sing to the Lord a new song. Let the people of Zion be glad.
O Lord, fill our mouths with praise and gratitude each and every day.

Thank You, Lord

Answered Prayers

Prayer Requests

Daybreak DEVOTIONS

DAY 39
DATE: _____

Song of Praise: "God Leads His Dear Children Along"

Disappointment Guaranteed

Throughout our entire life on this earth, we will experience disappointment. We will experience it through the people we look up to, the work environment, best friends, the church environment, and family. It comes to all of us. So welcome to life; it's just life. Disappointments come when our expectations are not met. This can leave a person angry, frustrated, and sad. It can create unhealed spiritual, mental, and emotional wounds. Physical wounds are easier to heal because they can be seen with the human eye. But spiritual, mental, and emotional wounds are unseen to the human eye, and only God can heal them.

God wants to heal us and make us whole. He wants to revitalize our faith and help us to get up, get over it, and move forward. He wants to release new faith, joy, and strength in us. He has a brighter future for us. This life guarantees disappointments, but His promise to us is beauty for ashes, the oil of joy for mourning, and the garment of praise for the spirit of heaviness.

"The Lord is good, a stronghold in the day of trouble." (Nahum 1:7a, KJV)

Daybreak Devotions

REFLECTIONS

Daybreak DEVOTIONS

PRAYER

In Daniel's prayer and confession, he says, "I set my face unto the Lord God, to seek by prayer and supplications, with fasting, and sackcloth, and ashes: And I prayed unto the Lord my God, and made my confession, and said, 'O Lord, the great and dreadful God, keeping covenant and mercy to them that love Him, and to them that keep His commandments.'" (Daniel 9:3-4)

O Lord, hear; O Lord, forgive: O, Lord, defer not, for thine own sake, for thy city and thy people are called by thy name. Amen. (Daniel 9:19)

Thank You, Lord

Answered Prayers

Prayer Requests

Daybreak DEVOTIONS

DAY 40
DATE: _____

Song of Praise: "I Am Delivered, Praise the Lord"

But If Not

When we are in the midst of a trial, our mindset is deliverance right away, but God always has our highest good in mind when He allows trials and tribulations to come our way. So, if God decides that deliverance from our trials is not necessarily our highest good, we must have the same faith position as the three Hebrew boys. That is "But if Not." This position of faith says our God is able to do this. "But if Not," we will still believe. This was the example of our Lord and Savior Jesus Christ recorded in St. Matthew 26:39 when He said, "Nevertheless." Job 13:15 gives us another example of "But if Not."

When he lost everything, his faith stood strong. We must accept that the Lord delivers some from trials and others in trials. We resolve to maintain a "But if Not" in our hearts and minds. He is a rewarder of faith that is unwavering.

"The Lord is my rock, and my fortress, and my deliverer." (2 Samuel 22:2, KJV)

Daybreak Devotions

REFLECTIONS

Daybreak DEVOTIONS

PRAYER

Father, in Jesus' name, we believe that some of us may be in the generation through which You want to bring to fruition Your great plans for the return of Your Son and the ushering in of Your glorious reign.

Our God and my Saviour, we realize there is a harvest to be gathered in; this is our hour to pray, believe God, and step up to the responsibility to which God has called the body of Christ, His Church. Father, make our lives count. Teach us how to overcome personal problems through faith and allow prayer to train and strengthen us for service in the kingdom. This is our prayer. Amen.

Thank You, Lord

Answered Prayers

Prayer Requests

Daybreak Devotions

DAY 41

DATE: _____

Song of Praise: "The King is Coming"

A Constant Readiness

What is our duty as believers? We find the answer in the words of St. Luke 19:11-13. These searching and impressive words found in these verses are "occupy until I come." These words will stir our spirit to examine ourselves and see if we are in constant readiness. As Christians, we are constantly preparing ourselves spiritually for the second coming of our Lord and Savior, Jesus Christ.

We must examine ourselves to see if we are constantly maintaining our faith position. Also, we must be "doing" believers. This means we are busy in the kingdom occupying until Jesus comes. When we are busy occupying ourselves, we will have no time for idle talking, gossiping, and a do-nothing religion. When busy occupying ourselves, it helps us to remain in constant readiness and become "doers." The work of the kingdom is how we let our light shine so that men may see our good works and glorify the Father who is in heaven. This will help us remain in constant readiness.

"Behold, the Lord cometh with ten thousand of His saints." (Jude 1:14b, KJV)

Daybreak Devotions

REFLECTIONS

Daybreak Devotions

PRAISE

Oh God, how wonderful You are! Your majesty, how bright. How beautiful Your mercy seat in the depths of burning light. How wonderful, how beautiful, the sight of Thee must be; You're endless; Your holiness is glorious. Your name is glorious. Your work is glorious. Your power is glorious. Your voice is glorious. Praise Ye the Lord!

Thank You, Lord

Answered Prayers

Prayer Requests

Daybreak Devotions

DAY 42

DATE: _____

Song of Praise: "Holy, Holy, Holy"

A Song in The Rain

"Birds" singing in the rain is a delightful sound. What is it that birds have from God that gives them a "song" in the rain? We, as human beings, are vulnerable, weak, and prone to complaining. We lose our ability to sing in the rain because we tend to focus on the negativity of rainfall. We complain instead of praising God for sending us the blessings of rain upon the earth. God, help us to have the devotion and discipline of the birds of the air. They are faithful every morning to sing unto the Lord at the breaking of the day. God, help us to have "bird sense." Help us to fill our mouths with praise every morning.

"My tongue shall speak thy praises all the day long." (Psalm 35:28, KJV)

Daybreak Devotions

REFLECTIONS

Daybreak DEVOTIONS

PRAYER

Father, set our affections on things above. Grant us the privilege to gaze upon You in adoration. Help us not to come into the Garden of Prayer unthinkingly and unpreparedly. Help us to honor Your presence, majesty, and glory when we approach You in prayer. Help our prayers to be sincere and from the heart. Let ineffective and powerless prayers be far from us. Create in us a clean heart and renew a right spirit. Help us reflect upon the greater riches of Your glory in Christ Jesus. Father, give us a glimpse of glory so we may pray the right prayers. In Your blessed name, we pray. Amen!

Thank You, Lord

Answered Prayers

Prayer Requests

Daybreak DEVOTIONS

DAY 43
DATE: _____

Song of Praise: "Hear Our Prayer, O Lord"

Strengthen Your Prayer Life

A prayer life is a bridge to bring us over many troubled waters. We cannot separate our lives from the blessings of prayer. Each depends upon the other because it is a part of a total life. There are times when we feel a loss of power in prayer, and our faith becomes weak. We have to search immediately within ourselves to see if there is any disobedience and sin lurking. All disobedience is a sin and will influence our prayer life. Nothing so quickly influences a prayer life as our relationship with other people. We cannot afford to sin against our brother or sister by thought, word, or deed. When that happens, we must go to God and our brother or sister and immediately ask for forgiveness. This strengthens our prayer life. God is always ready to forgive us and help us make things right without delay.

"For this shall everyone that is godly pray unto thee in a time when thou mayest be found." (Psalm 32:6, KJV)

Daybreak Devotions

REFLECTIONS

Daybreak DEVOTIONS

PRAYER

Our Father, who art in heaven, we are living in a time in which we desperately need answers outside the range of human possibilities. Man's extremity is God's opportunity. With God, nothing shall be impossible. As we seek You in prayer, we ask for Your wisdom, resources, and power to operate in remarkable ways. Thank You for filling our hearts with faith and expectation. We believe circumstances that have been presented in prayer are turning around. We expect a miraculous outcome because You're still the God of miracles. In Jesus' name, we pray. Amen! It is so!

Thank You, Lord

Answered Prayers

Prayer Requests

Daybreak DEVOTIONS

DAY 44

DATE: _____

Song of Praise: "God Will Take Care of You"

A Godly Home

A godly man will watch over his home and his family to establish godliness in the home. As loving leaders and priests of our home and family, we must set an example in everything we do. Our family, neighbors, community, and Christians are watching us. Our words should match the Christian life we live before our family and others. The eagle-eyed world watches behavior and words. A godly home is the best proof of true Christianity. A godly man must take care of his character in the home, for what we are there, we really are that wherever we go.

"It is no longer I that live, but Christ that liveth in me." (Galatians 2:20, KJV)

REFLECTIONS

Daybreak DEVOTIONS

PRAYER

Our Heavenly Father, You are a God who speaks. You are not like the gods of this world that cannot speak. You speak to us through Your creation, Your written Word through the Holy Spirit, and Your spoken Word will not return to You empty. We ask that You give us ears to hear and hearts to obey.

Keep our hearts sensitive to the Holy Spirit. Keep us full of spiritual life and keep us walking in truth and holiness. We pray that You keep us devoted to the Word of God and prayer. Father, fill us more fully with Your love, Your life, Your Holy Spirit, and Your fire. In Jesus' name, we pray. Amen!

Thank You, Lord

Answered Prayers

Prayer Requests

Daybreak Devotions

DAY 45

DATE: _____

Song of Praise: "Where He Leads Me"

Watchmen Upon the Walls

The call has gone out to the voices of intercessory prayer warriors. This is not the time to become passive prayer warriors in this current spiritual warfare climate. Just above our heads are operating principalities and powers fighting against us. Because of the intense spiritual warfare, the intercessory prayer warriors are being summoned to the place of prayer. Our prayer voices cannot be silent. Every church needs watchmen who will battle in prayer for families, homes, churches, and communities. 2 Chronicles 20:17a says to us today, "Ye shall not need to fight in this battle: set yourselves, stand ye still, and see the salvation of the Lord with you." Amen. And it is so.

"I have posted watchmen on your walls, Jerusalem; they will never be silent day or night. You who call on the Lord, give yourselves no rest." (Isaiah 62:6, KJV)

Daybreak Devotions

REFLECTIONS

Daybreak Devotions

PRAYER

Father, in Jesus' name, we come humbly before You, asking Your forgiveness and cleansing from sins of omission and sins of commission. Forgive us for thoughts, words, and deeds that have not pleased You. Have mercy upon us, most merciful Father - help us give ourselves more time in prayer. Stir us up to take hold of You in prayer mightily. Satan does not want us to pray. It is his business to choke down the Spirit of Prayer among the believers. But, Father, Your Son, Jesus, defeated him at Calvary's Cross. We thank You for a bold stand to pray through. Help us to come boldly unto the throne of grace, that we may obtain mercy and find grace to help in time of need. In Jesus' name, we pray. Amen.

Thank You, Lord

Answered Prayers

Prayer Requests

Daybreak DEVOTIONS

DAY 46
DATE: _____

Song of Praise: "As the Deer"

Victory Through Consistency

Consistency is the ability to be asserted together without contradictions. As we advance through life's challenges, our faith will bring us to levels of victory through the power of prayer and the Word of God. Our God is a God of consistency. This means He is a pattern of firmness, togetherness, harmony, and steady continuity.

We see the consistency of God in the creation of the universe, man, and angels. Even the movement of the earth, the planets, the stars, and the elements of nature display the consistency of God. They all work together harmoniously and in a steady uninterrupted, lasting connection of succession and union. God's purpose and plan for us is a life marked by faithfulness and consistency.

In these tough times filled with tough issues, we should ask God to help us to man up and woman up to face these perilous times with the good fight of faith, then march forward to claim victory through the power of consistency.

"And He is before all things, and by Him, all things consist." (Colossians 1:17, KJV)

Daybreak Devotions

REFLECTIONS

Daybreak DEVOTIONS

PRAYER

Our Father, who art in heaven, thank You for calling us to prayer through the unction of the Holy Spirit. We ask that You would help us to give ourselves to prayer. Father, You said in Your Word that if we ask anything according to Your will, You will hear us continually, and if we know that You hear us, whatsoever we ask, we know that we have the petitions that we desire of You. Thank You for hearing our asks, in Jesus' name. As we pray, God, You will work. As we pray, sinners are saved; as we pray, revival will come; as we pray, problems are solved; as we pray, the saints are encouraged and refreshed. We will pray! Amen.

Thank You, Lord

Answered Prayers

Prayer Requests

Daybreak Devotions

DAY 47

DATE: _____

Song of Praise: "Holy, Holy, Holy! Lord God Almighty"

Sensing God's Holiness

When we sense the holiness of God, it will move us to adore and magnify Him. Moses sensed the holiness of God at the burning bush when he was told to take his shoes off his feet for the place where he stood was holy ground. The basis and the goal of all God's requirements is His holy character. As His followers, we should be holy because we should reflect His character. He is our Father. He has created us and chosen us as His own. Therefore, we should be like Him. Also, we should be holy because He has determined to make us like Himself.

When we hear men trying to present their own holiness, they make light of the holiness of God. It is His holiness that we need to think and speak about. When we do that, we shall be prostate in the dust. A sight and sense of God's holiness are enough to show us how holy He is and how unholy we are.

"Holy, holy, holy Lord God Almighty, which was, and is, and is to come." (Revelation 4:8, KJV)

Daybreak Devotions

REFLECTIONS

Daybreak DEVOTIONS

PRAYER

Our Father and our God, we come boldly to the throne of grace. There, we can find mercy and grace to help. Thank You for being a very present help. Thank You for the Holy Spirit, the Comforter, the One called alongside to help us to pray. For we know not what we should pray for as we ought. But the Holy Spirit makes intercession for us through groanings that cannot be uttered. Father, we ask You to create in us an ear to hear what the Spirit has to say. Teach us how to listen to Your voice. Turn our minds toward You, Father, intentionally. Help us to learn how to sit quietly in Your presence and pay attention to what the Holy Spirit has to say to us, in Jesus' name. Amen.

Thank You, Lord

Answered Prayers

Prayer Requests

Daybreak DEVOTIONS

DAY 48
DATE: _____

Song of Praise: "Just a Closer Walk with Thee"

Never-the-Less

The word "nevertheless" means "in spite of," "howbeit," or "nonetheless." This adverb, with adjoining synonyms, is a way to express our faith and trust in the true and living God. During any severe testing time, believers must have a "nevertheless" mindset. This kind of thinking encourages us to remain stable in our faith and build a strong foundation of trust in the promises of God. In this thing called "life," we will encounter unstable times and situations. But a change is coming because light and life are in Jesus Christ. The test is for a testimony; the trial is to make us better and prepare us for future blessings. We have a future. Why? Because after a season of dimness, vexation, and darkness, there is a light at the end of the tunnel.

"Nevertheless" gives us confidence that we are coming out more than a conqueror. "Nevertheless" reassures us that God is in full control and this, too, shall work together for our good. Let's not be careless with our "nevertheless." Allow "nevertheless" to birth loyalty, kindness, endurance, joy, peace, temperance, goodness, and grace. Let's cherish the things God has deposited in us through our "nevertheless."

"Nevertheless, the foundation of God standeth sure, having this seal,
the Lord knoweth them that are his." (2 Timothy 2:19a, KJV)

Daybreak Devotions

REFLECTIONS

Daybreak DEVOTIONS

STEPS TOWARD SALVATION

1. Confess to God that you are a sinner and deserve death. "All have sinned and come short of the glory of God." (Romans 3:23)
2. "The wages of sin is death." (Romans 6:23)
3. In sorrow, turn from your sins to God and ask His forgiveness. "Let the wicked forsake his way, and the unrighteous man his thoughts, and let him return unto the Lord, and He will have mercy upon him, and He will abundantly pardon." (Isaiah 55:7)
4. "Believing that Christ died for our sins, was buried and that He rose again." (1 Corinthians 15:3-4)
5. "Trust Christ as Saviour and confess Him as Lord. If thou shalt confess with thy mouth the Lord, Jesus and shalt believe in thine heart that God hath raised him from the dead, thou shalt be saved." (Romans 10:9)
6. "Then Peter said unto them, repent, and be baptized every one of you. Then they that gladly received His Word were baptized." (Acts 2:38, 41)

Thank You, Lord

___

Answered Prayers

___

Prayer Requests

___

Daybreak Devotions

DAY 49

DATE: _____

Song of Praise: "Sweet Hour of Prayer"

Peaceful Sleep

There are different kinds of sleep. There is the sleep of the indolent or the lazy (Proverbs 6:9-11; 20:13; and 24:33-34). There is the sleep of the righteous (Proverbs 3:24-25 and Psalm 4:8).

Ministry and life's tests and trials can be exhausting. Jesus experienced exhaustion and found peaceful sleep in the hinder parts of a ship in a storm. He sleeps peacefully because He has been doing His Father's work. He sleeps peacefully because He has been doing and saying the right things. This gives Him a clean conscious. The conscious is the God part in us that touches our conduct, intentions, and character. Conscience is what convicts us of wrong and right. Conscience is a powerful thing. 1 Timothy 4:2 speaks of a conscience that can no longer discern between right and wrong. This is called a conscience seared with a hot iron. Hebrews 10:22 admonishes us to draw near to God with a true heart, allowing Him to cleanse our hearts from an evil conscience. Drug companies earn billions of dollars through sleep medications as a cure for insomnia. Our God gives us a prescription for peaceful sleep. We should treat people the way we want to be treated. Live a holy and separated life unto God. Don't let our good be evil spoken of. Shun the very appearance of evil. Don't dig ditches for other people.

We should not throw rocks and hide our hands. We should not sow discord among the brethren. We should be an example of the believer in conduct and speech and try to help somebody as we travel along the Christian way. We should love and appreciate family and friends, do an honest day's work, and when evening comes, we will lie down with a clear conscience and sleep peacefully.

"I will both lay me down in peace, and sleep: for thou, Lord, only makest me dwell in safety." (Psalm 4:8, KJV)

Daybreak Devotions

REFLECTIONS

Daybreak Devotions

PRAYER

Lord Jesus, You are coming again to this dark and sin-cursed world. We pray that You would send forth laborers into the harvest to prepare the hearts of men everywhere for Your return. O Savior, give us, as the servants of the most high God, willing hearts to go forth and work in Your vineyard. Help us to compel sinners to come to You for Your great salvation provided at Calvary's Cross. We need You more than ever. We pray that the fire of the Holy Ghost would ignite our hearts more in expectation of Your return. Even so, come, Lord Jesus! Help us to be ready! Amen.

Thank You, Lord

Answered Prayers

Prayer Requests

Daybreak DEVOTIONS

| DAY 50 |
| DATE: _____ |

Song of Praise: "Never Alone"

Refuse to Fear

Fear is the feeling of anticipated loss. In 1999, I had to taste the cup of being fearful due to the breakup of my marriage. I came face to face with fear. I felt frightened of the reality of being left alone after a very long married life. I became fearful that I would have to continue this journey called "life alone." After so many years of working together as a team, I was frightened of being left alone to carry the burden of ministry. Learning how to live and provide for myself without support was so unnerving. But, thank God, the Holy Spirit reminded me of God's promise never to leave nor forsake me.

My faith was recharged through prayer and the promises of God in His Word. During those hours, days, weeks, months, and years, prayer became the anchor of my soul. God, who is faithful, brought me out more than a conqueror.

Beloved, as you read this final day of devotion, know that God will help you conquer your fears as well. Since He did it for me, He will do the same for you. Just trust Him and never doubt."

"For God has not given us a spirit of fear, but of power and love and of a sound mind." (2Timothy 1:7, KJV)

Daybreak Devotions

REFLECTIONS

Daybreak DEVOTIONS

PRAYER

Father, in the name of Jesus Christ our Lord, as believers, we join together in united and persevering prayer and wait patiently for You to fulfill Your promise. Thank You for a fresh outpouring of the Holy Spirit to help us to become living testimonies. Help us to grow in maturity under the leadership of Your apostles, prophets, pastors, teachers, and evangelists. As we submit ourselves to Your holy and divine will in humility, simplicity and integrity, we pray that the world will see the reflection of Jesus Christ our Lord. Thank You because You have not given us the spirit of fear but of love, power, and a sound mind. We will not fear but have faith in Your mighty name. Amen.

Thank You, Lord

Answered Prayers

Prayer Requests